THE
MAKER'S
DIET

DAY-BY-DAY JOURNAL

JORDAN S. RUBIN

SILOAM
A STRANG COMPANY

Most Strang Communications/Charisma House/Siloam products are available at special quantity discounts for bulk purchase for sales promotions, premiums, fund-raising, and educational needs. For details, write Strang Communications/Charisma House/Siloam, 600 Rinehart Road, Lake Mary, Florida 32746, or telephone (407) 333-0600.

The Maker's Diet Day-by-Day Journal
by Jordan Rubin

Published by Siloam
A Strang Company
600 Rinehart Road
Lake Mary, Florida 32746
www.siloam.com

Cover design by
Koechel Peterson & Associates,
Minneapolis, MN
Interior design by Terry Clifton

Library of Congress Control Number: 2004111838
International Standard Book Number:
1-59185-620-5

05 06 07 08—987654321
Printed in the United States of America

Introduction

Nearly ten years ago I found myself suffering from an incurable illness: Crohn's disease. After visiting what seemed like every doctor on the planet and trying every "miracle" drug, "miracle" diet, and "miracle" supplement—and finding no help—I began tearing through the pages of the world's oldest, most sacred, and best-selling book.

What I was looking for in the Bible was not purely spiritual. *I was looking for answers to my many debilitating health problems.* What I found was man's first health plan—and the *only* health program I will need for the rest of my life. This ancient health program literally transformed the life of a seemingly hopeless twenty-year-old, and since I first wrote about it, thousands of people have used these same principles to pull themselves out of the grip of disease and enter the promised land of health.

The Maker's Diet Day-by-Day Journal is the essential companion to my book, *The Maker's Diet*. The *Day-by-Day Journal* helps you track your progress through the three phases of the Maker's Diet. I designed it to be small and portable, perfect to slip in your purse or pocket, so you'll be able to keep track of your meals and exercise.

I've provided two-page spreads for you to track all forty days of the plan. You have space to record your hygiene, your meals and snacks, and your exercise. Each day also includes a helpful quote from *The Maker's Diet* and an encouraging Scripture verse, as well as places to mark that you've had your morning and evening prayer.

I'm also excited to provide the fitness section and charts. Here I've included information from *The Maker's Diet* on the benefits of simple exercises, like walking, rebounding, and even deep breathing. The charts give you a place to track your progress through the three phases. And because this book is such a handy size, you can throw it in your gym bag or keep it in your pocket as you walk.

Remember, the consequences of 3 your health choices will affect many more people than yourself. You owe it to yourself and everyone you care about to return to the Maker's Diet. I hope this book will help you find success on the plan.

A morning prayer for healing

Father God, I thank You for creating me in Your image. I praise You that I am fearfully and wonderfully made. I confess that You are the God who heals, my Great Physician. I ask You to heal my body from the top of my head to the soles of my feet. I pray that You would regenerate every bone, joint, tendon, ligament, tissue, organ, and cell of my body. This is the day that the Lord has made; I will rejoice and be glad in it. Amen.

An evening prayer for restoration

Father God, I thank You for sustaining me today. I thank You that You are made perfect in my weakness. Your grace is sufficient for me. I thank You that Your steadfast love never ceases and Your mercies are new every morning. You say in Your Word that mourning may come for a night, but the new day will bring gladness. Bless me with a healing night's sleep. Restore unto me the joy of my salvation. Help me to stay on the path that leads to life. Amen.

THE MAKER'S DIET

I'm convinced that the Creator knew what He was doing when He created us, and I believe His Word is the foundation for total health: spiritual, mental, and emotional, as well as physical.

○ *Morning Prayer*

Hygiene

Breakfast

Lunch

Dinner

Snack

Exercise and Fitness

○ *Evening Prayer*

I waited patiently for the LORD;
And He inclined unto me,
And heard my cry.
He also brought me up out of a
horrible pit,
Out of the miry clay,
And set my feet upon a rock,
And established my steps.
He has put a new song in my mouth—
Praise to our God;
Many will see it and fear,
And will trust in the LORD.
                              —PSALM 40:1–3, NKJV

THE MAKER'S DIET

> *Diets and health fads litter the land-scape of American culture, but the Maker's original plan for your optimal health and wellness is no fad.*

○ *Morning Prayer*

Hygiene

Breakfast

Lunch

Dinner

Snack

Exercise and Fitness

○ *Evening Prayer*

In thee, O LORD, do I put my trust....Bow down thine ear to me; deliver me speedily....I will be glad and rejoice in thy mercy: for thou hast considered my trouble.

—PSALM 31:1–2, 7

THE MAKER'S DIET

> *Tackle your forty-day experience with a friend or a whole group of friends. This program is ideally undertaken in a small-group setting.*

○ *Morning Prayer*
Hygiene
Breakfast
Lunch

Dinner

Snack

Exercise and Fitness

○ *Evening Prayer*

Have mercy upon me, O LORD, for *I am in trouble:* mine eye is consumed with grief, yea, my soul *and my belly.*
—PSALM 31:9, EMPHASIS ADDED

THE MAKER'S DIET

> *If you want to experience real results in your life, it will take some determination on your part—but achieving your dream of superb health is a worthwhile goal.*

◯ *Morning Prayer*
Hygiene
Breakfast
Lunch

Dinner

Snack

Exercise and Fitness

○ *Evening Prayer*

Make thy face to shine upon thy
servant: save me for thy mercies'
sake....Blessed be the LORD: for he
hath shewed me his marvellous kind-
ness in a strong city.

—PSALM 31:16, 21

THE MAKER'S DIET

Make time for fun. I recommend at least one day per week to be a fun day. Don't do anything that resembles work.

○ *Morning Prayer*
Hygiene
Breakfast
Lunch

Dinner

Snack

Exercise and Fitness

○ *Evening Prayer*

Rejoice in the Lord always. I will say it again: Rejoice!
—PHILIPPIANS 4:4, NIV

THE MAKER'S DIET

> *If you usually eat "on the run," choose
> to sit down when you eat, and turn off
> the television or radio.*

○ *Morning Prayer*
Hygiene
Breakfast
Lunch

Dinner

Snack

Exercise and Fitness

❍ ***Evening Prayer***

I will extol thee, O LORD; for thou hast lifted me up, and hast not made my foes to rejoice over me. O LORD my God, I cried unto thee, and thou hast healed me. O LORD, thou hast brought up my soul from the grave: thou hast kept me alive, that I should not go down to the pit.

—PSALM 30:1–3

THE MAKER'S DIET

The wisdom in our physiology and biochemistry cry out for a primitive, biblical diet with plentiful amounts of healthy meat, fish, fruit, vegetables, dairy, and nuts.

○ *Morning Prayer*

Hygiene

Breakfast

Lunch

Dinner

Snack

Exercise and Fitness

○ *Evening Prayer*

Thou hast turned for me my mourning into dancing: thou hast put off my sackcloth, and girded me with gladness; to the end that my glory may sing praise to thee, and not be silent. O LORD my God, I will give thanks unto thee for ever.

—PSALM 30:11–12

THE MAKER'S DIET

> *I am convinced that we help create many of our problems through wrong thinking, poor decision making, and poor dietary choices.*

○ *Morning Prayer*
Hygiene
Breakfast
Lunch

Dinner

Snack

Exercise and Fitness

○ *Evening Prayer*

For as he thinketh in his heart, so is he: Eat and drink, saith he to thee; but his heart is not with thee.

—PROVERBS 23:7

THE MAKER'S DIET

> *Music is a gift from God that possesses*
> *healing and delivering powers.*

○ *Morning Prayer*

Hygiene

Breakfast

Lunch

Dinner

Snack

Exercise and Fitness

○ *Evening Prayer*

Also seven priests shall carry seven trumpets of rams' horns before the ark; then on the seventh day you shall march around the city seven times, and the priests shall blow the trumpets. It shall be that when they make a long blast with the ram's horn, and when you hear the sound of the trumpet, all the people shall shout with a great shout; and the wall of the city will fall down flat, and the people will go up every man straight ahead.

—JOSHUA 6:4–5, NAS

THE MAKER'S DIET

> *Exposure to sunlight can be very beneficial for your health and can aid in the balance of hormones, enhance mood, and help to build strong bones.*

○ *Morning Prayer*
Hygiene
Breakfast
Lunch

Dinner

Snack

Exercise and Fitness

◯ *Evening Prayer*

H is splendor covers the heavens,
And the earth is full of His praise.
His radiance is like the sunlight;
He has rays flashing from His hand.
—HABAKKUK 3:3–4, NAS

THE MAKER'S DIET

> *Faith is not just something you say—
> it is something you live, moment by
> moment.*

◗ *Morning Prayer*
Hygiene
Breakfast
Lunch

Dinner

Snack

Exercise and Fitness

○ *Evening Prayer*

Without faith it is impossible to please God, because anyone who comes to him must believe that he exists and that he rewards those who earnestly seek him.

—HEBREWS 11:6, NIV

THE MAKER'S DIET

> *If you mess up and go off the program,
> do not beat yourself up! You are only
> one meal away from success.*

○ *Morning Prayer*

Hygiene

Breakfast

Lunch

Dinner

Snack

Exercise and Fitness

○ *Evening Prayer*

"For I know the plans I have for you," declares the LORD, "plans to prosper you and not to harm you, plans to give you hope and a future."
—JEREMIAH 29:11, NIV

THE MAKER'S DIET

> *The best way to "cure" disease is to never get it.*

○ *Morning Prayer*

Hygiene

Breakfast

Lunch

Dinner

Snack

Exercise and Fitness

○ *Evening Prayer*

If you diligently heed the voice of the LORD your God...I will put none of these diseases on you, which I have brought on the Egyptians. I am the LORD who heals you.

—EXODUS 15:26, NKJV

THE MAKER'S DIET

> *I believe that faith and positive thinking, based on God's Word, are vital keys to recovering and maintaining health.*

○ *Morning Prayer*

Hygiene

Breakfast

Lunch

Dinner

Snack

Exercise and Fitness

○ *Evening Prayer*

Faith is the substance of things hoped for, the evidence of things not seen.

—HEBREWS 11:1, NKJV

THE MAKER'S DIET

> *I am thankful for science and human advances in medicine and nutrition, but where science presumes to dismiss the Creator's foundational principles, I am convinced His pattern provides us with a better approach to life.*

○ **Morning Prayer**
Hygiene
Breakfast
Lunch

Dinner

Snack

Exercise and Fitness

○ *Evening Prayer*

For who hath known the mind of the Lord, that he may instruct him? But we have the mind of Christ.

—1 CORINTHIANS 2:16

THE MAKER'S DIET

> *When I started to believe I was well and to give thanks to God for the moments of well-being I experienced, I began to get well.*

○ *Morning Prayer*

Hygiene

Breakfast

Lunch

Dinner

Snack

Exercise and Fitness

○ *Evening Prayer*

Go thy way; and as thou hast believed, so be it done unto thee.
—MATTHEW 8:13

THE MAKER'S DIET

> *Even if you don't exercise at all, you can
> begin to improve your health immedi-
> ately by starting to exercise now.*

○ *Morning Prayer*
Hygiene
Breakfast
Lunch

Dinner

Snack

Exercise and Fitness

○ *Evening Prayer*

For what shall it profit a man, if he shall gain the whole world, and lose his own soul? Or what shall a man give in exchange for his soul?

—MARK 8:36–37, NKJV

THE MAKER'S DIET

> *You should prepare lists of your favor-*
> *ite music, and then play the music*
> *often. See if it doesn't lift your spirits.*

○ *Morning Prayer*

Hygiene

Breakfast

Lunch

Dinner

Snack

Exercise and Fitness

○ *Evening Prayer*

And it came to pass, when the evil spirit from God was upon Saul, that David took an harp, and played with his hand: so Saul was refreshed, and was well, and the evil spirit departed from him.

—1 SAMUEL 16:23

THE MAKER'S DIET

> *My mission in life since my recovery is
> to help people who are sick regain their
> health and to help the healthy flourish
> even more.*

◯ *Morning Prayer*

Hygiene

Breakfast

Lunch

Dinner

Snack

Exercise and Fitness

○ *Evening Prayer*

Beloved, I wish above all things that thou mayest prosper and be in health, even as thy soul prospereth.

—3 JOHN 2

THE MAKER'S DIET

Despite our technological advancements, our physical bodies are still designed to consume and thrive on the same foods in the same proportions that our primitive ancestors ate thousands of years ago!

○ *Morning Prayer*

Hygiene

Breakfast

Lunch

Dinner

Snack

Exercise and Fitness

○ *Evening Prayer*

And God said, Behold, I have given you every herb bearing seed, which is upon the face of all the earth, and every tree, in the which is the fruit of a tree yielding seed; to you it shall be for meat.

—GENESIS 1:29

THE MAKER'S DIET

> *In most cases, the things you do and
> say begin with the things you think and
> believe.*

◯ *Morning Prayer*

Hygiene

Breakfast

Lunch

Dinner

Snack

Exercise and Fitness

○ *Evening Prayer*

But those things which proceed out of the mouth come forth from the heart; and they defile the man.
—MATTHEW 15:18

THE MAKER'S DIET

> *I am convinced the Creator's prescription for exercise more closely resembles real-life activities involved in the daily patterns of work and play.*

◐ *Morning Prayer*
Hygiene
Breakfast
Lunch

Dinner

Snack

Exercise and Fitness

○ *Evening Prayer*

And whatsoever ye do, do it heart-
ily, as to the Lord, and not unto men.
—COLOSSIANS 3:23

THE MAKER'S DIET

> *The biggest problems with modern dairy products come from our habit of "tinkering" with dairy animals and their milk products to "make them better."*

○ *Morning Prayer*
Hygiene
Breakfast
Lunch

Dinner

Snack

Exercise and Fitness

○ *Evening Prayer*

When I gave my heart to know wisdom...and I saw every work of God, I concluded that man cannot discover the work which has been done under the sun. Even though man should seek laboriously, he will not discover.

—ECCLESIASTES 8:16–17, NAS

THE MAKER'S DIET

> *If we ever hope to be counted among the world's healthiest people, we must leave behind our disease-producing diets and lifestyle and return to our Creator's dietary guidelines, as incorporated in the Maker's Diet!*

○ *Morning Prayer*

Hygiene

Breakfast

Lunch

Dinner

Snack

Exercise and Fitness

○ *Evening Prayer*

And I heard another voice from heaven, saying, Come out of her, my people, that ye be not partakers of her sins, and that ye receive not of her plagues.

—REVELATION 18:4

THE MAKER'S DIET

> *Is it really worth the dangerous cost to hold on to anger or unforgiveness? Are we really willing to destroy ourselves in a quest for revenge?*

○ *Morning Prayer*

Hygiene

Breakfast

Lunch

Dinner

Snack

Exercise and Fitness

○ *Evening Prayer*

For if ye forgive men their trespasses, your heavenly Father will also forgive you: But if ye forgive not men their trespasses, neither will your Father forgive your trespasses.

—MATTHEW 6:14–15

THE MAKER'S DIET

> *God created us to live, move, work, play, overcome obstacles, and win victories throughout life. He never intended for us to sit around and wait for death.*

○ *Morning Prayer*
Hygiene
Breakfast
Lunch

Dinner

Snack

Exercise and Fitness

○ *Evening Prayer*

For we are his workmanship, created in Christ Jesus unto good works, which God hath before ordained that we should walk in them.

—EPHESIANS 2:10

THE MAKER'S DIET

> *History has proven that the body can heal itself from many serious conditions by fasting, and today the healthcare community is beginning to catch on.*

◑ Morning Prayer

Hygiene

Breakfast

Lunch

Dinner

Snack

Exercise and Fitness

○ *Evening Prayer*

But godliness actually is a means of great gain when accompanied by contentment.

—1 TIMOTHY 6:6, NAS

THE MAKER'S DIET

A brisk two-mile walk (with long strides and vigorous arm movement) every day increases enzyme and metabolic activity and may increase calorie burning for up to twelve hours afterward!

○ *Morning Prayer*

Hygiene

Breakfast

Lunch

Dinner

Snack

Exercise and Fitness

○ *Evening Prayer*

Do you not know that those who run in a race all run, but only one receives the prize? Run in such a way that you may win.

—1 CORINTHIANS 9:24, NAS

THE MAKER'S DIET

> *Get proper rest. There is simply no substitute for quality sleep....Sleep is so vital to health that I often refer to it as the most important non-nutrient you can get.*

○ *Morning Prayer*

Hygiene

Breakfast

Lunch

Dinner

Snack

Exercise and Fitness

◯ *Evening Prayer*

W hen thou liest down, thou shalt
not be afraid: yea, thou shalt lie down,
and thy sleep shall be sweet.

—PROVERBS 3:24

THE MAKER'S DIET

> *I recommend conversation with good friends during meals or reading something uplifting, such as God's Word.*

○ *Morning Prayer*
Hygiene
Breakfast
Lunch

Dinner

Snack

Exercise and Fitness

○ *Evening Prayer*

And these words, which I command thee this day, shall be in thine heart: And thou shalt teach them diligently unto thy children, and shalt talk of them when thou sittest in thine house, and when thou walkest by the way, and when thou liest down, and when thou risest up.

—Deuteronomy 6:6–7

THE MAKER'S DIET

> *It seems the state of our health as a nation is worse than ever before. Today, nearly 65 percent of American adults are overweight, and almost 30 percent are obese.[1]*

○ *Morning Prayer*

Hygiene

Breakfast

Lunch

Dinner

Snack

Exercise and Fitness

○ *Evening Prayer*

Why do you spend money for
what...does not satisfy?
Listen carefully to Me, and eat what
is good,
And delight yourself in abundance.
—ISAIAH 55:2, NAS

THE MAKER'S DIET

> *Unmanaged stress can kill you. It may*
> *be the single most important "trigger"*
> *of heart attacks.*

○ *Morning Prayer*

Hygiene

Breakfast

Lunch

Dinner

Snack

Exercise and Fitness

◯ *Evening Prayer*

A merry heart doeth good like a medicine: but a broken spirit drieth the bones.

—PROVERBS 17:22

THE MAKER'S DIET

> *I will spend the rest of my life telling the*
> *world the truth that will set them free.*

◯ *Morning Prayer*

Hygiene

Breakfast

Lunch

Dinner

Snack

Exercise and Fitness

○ *Evening Prayer*

And ye shall know the truth, and
the truth shall make you free.
—JOHN 8:32

THE MAKER'S DIET

> *God's dietary guidelines are not some narrow-minded religious exercise meant to set apart certain people from their neighbors. They were given by a loving God to save His people from physical devastation.*

○ *Morning Prayer*
Hygiene
Breakfast
Lunch

Dinner

Snack

Exercise and Fitness

○ *Evening Prayer*

$\mathbf{M}$y people are destroyed for lack of knowledge.

—HOSEA 4:6, NAS

THE MAKER'S DIET

> *A wealth of nutrition awaits hurting bodies that are fed liberal doses of fruits, vegetables, herbs, lentils, and properly prepared whole grains (along with the meat, fish, and dairy products introduced later by the Creator).*

○ *Morning Prayer*
Hygiene
Breakfast
Lunch

Dinner

Snack

Exercise and Fitness

○ *Evening Prayer*

Every moving thing that liveth shall be meat for you; even as the green herb have I given you all things.
—GENESIS 9:3

THE MAKER'S DIET

> *Our Creator established our genetic and nutritional requirements long ago.*

◯ *Morning Prayer*
Hygiene
Breakfast
Lunch

Dinner

Snack

Exercise and Fitness

○ *Evening Prayer*

Y̶ou formed my inward parts;
You wove me in my mother's womb.
I will give thanks to You, for I am
    fearfully and wonderfully made;
Wonderful are Your works,
And my soul knows it very well.
                    —PSALM 139:13–14, NAS

THE MAKER'S DIET

> *If you feel overwhelmed by the stresses of the day, I recommend that you listen to your favorite worship music and join in.*

○ *Morning Prayer*
Hygiene
Breakfast
Lunch

Dinner

Snack

Exercise and Fitness

○ *Evening Prayer*

I will also praise You with a harp,
Even Your truth, O my God;
To You I will sing praises with the lyre,
O Holy One of Israel.
My lips will shout for joy when I sing
   praises to You;
And my soul, which You have
   redeemed.

—PSALM 71:22–23, NAS

THE MAKER'S DIET

> A seemingly far-fetched, ridiculous-sounding, positive thought, word, or action that you can choose to express in your moment of desperation can act as a seed of faith that will spark the healing process for you.

◗ *Morning Prayer*
Hygiene
Breakfast
Lunch

Dinner

Snack

Exercise and Fitness

○ *Evening Prayer*

Verily I say unto you, If ye have faith as a grain of mustard seed, ye shall say unto this mountain, Remove hence to yonder place; and it shall remove; and nothing shall be impossible unto you.
—MATTHEW 17:20

THE MAKER'S DIET

> *Besides giving us the night for regular sleep, the Creator programmed people and animals to rest completely every seventh day.*

○ *Morning Prayer*

Hygiene

Breakfast

Lunch

Dinner

Snack

Exercise and Fitness

○ *Evening Prayer*

Six days shall work be done: but the seventh day is the sabbath of rest, an holy convocation; ye shall do no work therein: it is the sabbath of the LORD in all your dwellings.

—LEVITICUS 23:3

THE MAKER'S DIET

> *We are much less active than we used to be, but even a little exercise goes a long way.*

○ *Morning Prayer*

Hygiene

Breakfast

Lunch

Dinner

Snack

Exercise and Fitness

○ *Evening Prayer*

H ow long wilt thou sleep, O slug-
gard? when wilt thou arise out of thy
sleep?

—PROVERBS 6:9

Fitness

God created us to *live, move, work, play, overcome obstacles,* and *win victories* throughout life. He never intended for us to sit around and wait for death.

Some confirmed couch potatoes have confidently justified their lackadaisical approach to life by quoting the passage from the King James Bible, "For bodily exercise profiteth little" (1 Tim. 4:8). They conveniently forget that Timothy probably walked everywhere he went and got more exercise in one day than most people do today in a week. Modern translations more accurately paint the picture and remove the "lazy boy loophole," saying, "For physical training is *of some value*" (1 Tim. 4:8, NIV, emphasis added).

What Was It You Were Waiting for Again?

We have a world to explore and master, and we can't do it if our bodies are accumulating fat, and our muscles, joints, and internal organs are breaking down. We all need exercise.

For about three decades, the extended-exertion theory of aerobic exercise has ruled supreme in medical and physical fitness circles. This theory maintains that maximum health comes from exercising the cardiovascular system to elevated or maximum stress levels for *sustained or unbroken time periods* (usually thirty minutes or more). The belief is that this trains or strengthens the cardiovascular system much as a bodybuilder exercises muscles through applied stress to achieve maximum size or strength.

This may be true; however, the weakness of this theory comes from its foundation in the flawed "clogged artery/high cholesterol" theories of cardiovascular disease. Lower cholesterol rates have no connection with lower incidences of heart attack or heart disease; it is better to use the genuinely accurate homocysteine levels and oxidative stress as risk factors.[1]

Unfortunately, the stressful and artificial nature of sustained aerobic exercises has worn out joints and cartilage and inflicted serious chronic sports injuries at rates higher than anyone predicted. Even worse, aerobically fit people with low cholesterol levels are dropping dead from heart attacks just as often as those who *never* exercise and have terrible cholesterol levels. This may be due to the fact that people who regularly perform aerobic exercise for long periods of time experience a weakened immune system. This drop in immunity makes them prime targets for infections.

We *do* need exercise for maximum health, but high-stress aerobic exercise just doesn't seem to be delivering as promised.

Exercise Should Mirror Real Life

From my research, I am convinced the Creator's prescription for exercise more closely resembles real-life activities involved in the daily patterns of work and play.

The longest-lived peoples in human history usually walked everywhere they went, trailed their animals and herds, hunted wild game on foot, built rugged shelters, or cultivated fields at an active pace each day with intermittent periods of rest. They knew *nothing* about aerobic exercise, treadmills, or running tracks, but they were masters at *anaerobic exercise*—activities that incur an "oxygen debt" through temporary or briefly sustained exertion.

Current fashion fads aside, we don't need to look as muscular as the people we see on television or on magazine covers, but *anyone* can certainly be a lot healthier with a nutritious diet and moderate exercise.

I am not completely against aerobic exercise, but if your goal is to live a healthier life free of disease and needless health complications, there are certain exercises that are much better for your overall health.

Walking

My description of the oldest physical activity of the human race can be expressed in one word: *walking*. Even before Eve, Adam was assigned the task to care for God's garden—a job that could not be done without *walking*. Subsequent development of our species demanded even more walking.

A brisk two-mile walk (with long strides and vigorous arm movement) every day increases enzyme and metabolic activity and may increase calorie burning for up to twelve hours afterward![2]

Don't waste time looking for choice parking spots *close* to your destination—choose a spot *far away* and *walk* there. This takes care of two important priorities at once—you get what you came for, *and* you're getting healthful exercise, too! (And forget the elevators and escalators—take the stairs.) Take a walk on the beach or to the corner store; just don't buy junk food for the return trip. Ride a bicycle, stroll through your neighborhood, and "walk the mall" when the weather doesn't cooperate.

Functional Fitness

Functional fitness is a system of exercise that is truly holistic. Functional fitness utilizes movements that are natural to the body; it enhances the health and strength of every muscle. Unlike traditional bodybuilding, functional training focuses on improving the strength of the body's core (the abdominals and lower back), which also houses many of our most important organs.

Functional fitness can be used to achieve great results by people of all walks of life, from the professional athlete who wants to improve performance to the grandmother who wants to climb the stairs to her bedroom more easily. Functional training (fitness) expert Juan Carlos Santana says it best: "Function is a duty or purpose of a thing—or what something is intended for. One of the main things that the body is intended for is to provide structure and movement. Therefore, functional training (fitness) would be any training that enhances the body's structure and/or movement."[3]

There is no doubt in my mind that *functional fitness* is the most effective exercise and fitness system available. I feel it truly deserves to be used officially as the Functional Fitness Exercise Program.

Even deep-breathing exercises will increase the fat-burning metabolism of your body and "boost your brain" with a rich dose of oxygen. Deep breathing offers benefits that might make a major difference in your health. Your lungs are larger at the bottom than at the top, but most people in America are "top breathers." We live on the shallow breaths common to the sick and the sleeping.

Learn to breathe "from the gut." You know you are breathing from the diaphragm if you see your stomach move in and out. If the only thing that moves or expands is your chest, then you are still living on a shallow percentage of the divine potential for deep breathing.

Deep breathing literally "massages" and moves the soft internal organs inside your rib cage, allowing your lymph system to rid itself of collected toxins and to collect even more. Only deep breathing allows you to tap the "bonus power" of your lower lungs.

Newborn babies *instinctively* deep breathe—watch and learn at the next opportunity. We actually "learn" how to "shallow breathe" and rob ourselves of the breath of life. Singers, stage performers, broadcast announcers, and professional athletes pay great sums to voice coaches and breathing coaches to learn how to breathe, project the voice, and achieve maximum strength through diaphragm breathing (which is what they did *naturally* as babies). Here is a quick course just to get you started:

1. Sit or lie down and relax.
2. Place a hand your abdomen to see if it expands as you breathe. If only your chest moves with your breaths, you are "shallow breathing."
3. Breathe deeply through your mouth, and breathe "all the way down to your belly button." Your abdomen (stomach) should rise as you inhale (not your chest).
4. Hold your breath for a few seconds, and then exhale slowly and fully. Learn to recognize the sounds and sensations of long, slow, deep breaths as your Maker intended.[4]

With more practice, you will revert back to the instinctive deep-breathing way you began life.

Rebounding

One way to get the exercise you need is *rebounding*, in which you use a portable mini-trampoline to jog, jump, hop, twist, or step walk in place. One respected advocate of rebounding uses the devices and rebounding techniques in his rehabilitation program. According to James White, PhD, director of research and rehabilitation in the physical education department of the University of California at San Diego (UCSD), "When you jump, jog and twist on this [rebounding] device, you can exercise for hours without getting tired. It's great practice for skiing, it improves your tennis stroke, and it's a good way to burn off calories and lose weight."[5] Dr. White believes it is more effective for fitness and weight loss than cycling, running, or jogging—while producing fewer injuries.

If you are stuck indoors, try some "rebounding" exercise in which you jump on a mini-trampoline. Rebounding is very good for the lymphatic system, the circulatory system, and the spine (while sparing your joints and ligaments).

Even a little helps

We are much less active than we used to be, but even a little exercise goes a long way. An article in *Consumer Reports on Health* described a study of 13,000 men and women at the Cooper Institute for Aerobics Research in Dallas, Texas. The researchers conducted the eight-year study hoping to prove the value of consistent aerobic exercise, based on how long the volunteers could stand to exercise on a treadmill.

> As fitness increased, the death rate fell. But by far, the *biggest drop in mortality*—60 percent for men, nearly 50 percent for the women—occurred between *the most unfit volunteers* and *those who were just slightly more fit.*[6]

Regardless of where you land on the exercise scale, this should make you feel better. Even if you don't exercise at all, you can begin to improve your health immediately by starting to exercise *now*.

I hope this chapter has served as a "tune-up," a service warning light on your health dashboard. Even if you faithfully follow the guidelines and food recommendations of *The Maker's Diet*, you will need to practice the philosophy of "stop, drop, and roll" on a regular basis.

Don't wait until you smell smoke—learn to read your body's symptoms and discern the familiar warning signs. At the first sign of fire or flames burning where they shouldn't be, stop everything to *rest, fast, and exercise* a little. It doesn't take much to recharge your battery.

Even when you are trying to do everything right, there may be those times when you need some of the Maker's medicine. Fortunately for us, He has supplied them in abundance. In the rigors of daily life, you may need to take a hot/cold shower, anoint yourself with essential oils, listen to music that soothes the soul, and allow the warmth of a hot bath soak deep into your aching bones. This may seem like a description for a day at the spa—but it's just biblical medicine.

Using the Charts

The charts provided here allow you to track your fitness progress through the three phases. For each day, mark which of the exercises you did and for how long. Go for it!

THE <u>MAKER'S</u> <u>DIET</u> DAY-BY-DAY JOURNAL

EXERCISE		DAY 1	2	3	4	5	6	7	8	9	10	11	12	13	PHASE ONE 14
WALKING	YES / NO														
	TIME														
REBOUNDING	YES / NO														
	TIME														
DEEP BREATHING	YES / NO														
	TIME														
FUNCTIONAL FITNESS	YES / NO														
	TIME														

			DAY										PHASE TWO		
EXERCISE		15	16	17	18	19	20	21	22	23	24	25	26	27	28
WALKING	YES / NO														
	TIME														
REBOUNDING	YES / NO														
	TIME														
DEEP BREATHING	YES / NO														
	TIME														
FUNCTIONAL FITNESS	YES / NO														
	TIME														

Workout Log

THE MAKER'S DIET DAY-BY-DAY JOURNAL

PHASE THREE

EXERCISE		DAY 29	30	31	32	33	34	35	36	37	38	39	40		
WALKING	YES / NO														
	TIME														
REBOUNDING	YES / NO														
	TIME														
DEEP BREATHING	YES / NO														
	TIME														
FUNCTIONAL FITNESS	YES / NO														
	TIME														

Conclusion

The Maker's Diet 40-Day Health Experience incorporates the same biblical dietary and lifestyle principles that saved my life, and I hope *The Maker's Diet Day-by-Day Journal* helps you in your own journey to wellness. As a result of my years of research and experience with patients, I estimate *it is at least ten times as effective* as the early version of the program that I used to regain my health and break free from the bondage of disease!

As of this writing, I have been off all medications for nine years and am extremely healthy. After suffering the ravages of continuous exposure to powerful medications, including catabolic steroids, for years, I have regained my normal weight (195 pounds at 6 feet 1 inch). I work out, play recreational sports, and am happily married with a family. I am still awed by this miracle, considering that I used to wonder if I would *live long enough* to see my twenty-first birthday.

If an injection, pill, or experimental therapy could have freed me from my painful disease, I would have paid any amount of money to get it. (And we *did* spend hundreds of thousands of dollars in our futile search for a cure.)

God definitely healed me, but He did it in the natural, practical way I have shared with you—through the Maker's Diet. My mother says it best; I was healed "as I feasted on the Word of God" and applied His principles—including dietary—to my life. Believe me, these principles of divine health are completely reproducible in your life, too.

Notes

Day 31

1. Statistics Related to Overweight and Obesity, NIDDK Weight-Control Information Network, http://www.niddk.nih.gov/health/nutrit/pubs/statobes.htm#other (accessed November 5, 2003).

Fitness

1. Sally Fallon, with Mary G. Enig, PhD, *Nourishing Traditions* (Washington, D.C.: New Trends Publishing, Inc., 1999), 13, citing J. B. Ubbink, *Nutr Rev* 52 (November 1994): 383–393.

2. Paul Chek, "The Power of Walking," C.H.E.K. Institute, http://www.chekinstitute.com/articles.cfm?select=38 (accessed June 14, 2003).

3. Juan Carlos Santana, M.Ed., CSCS, "The 4 Pillars of Human Movement: A Movement Approach to Exercise Design and Implementation," http://www.canfitpro.com/html/documents/Santana-The4PillarsofHumanMovement.doc (accessed November 30, 2003).

4. For detailed information about the benefits and methods to instill deep breathing patterns, see Davis, Eshelman, and McKay, *The Relaxation and Stress Reduction Notebook*, 2nd ed. (New Harbringer Publications, 1982).

5. Morton Walker, DPM, "Jumping for Health," *Townsend Letter for Doctors* (n.d.).

6. Mark and Patti Virkler, *Eden's Health Plan—Go Natural!* (Shippensburg, PA: Destiny Image Publishers, 1994), 132, citing "Exercise: A Little Helps a Lot," *Consumer Reports on Health*, volume 6, number 8 (August 1994), 89.

Strang Communications, the publisher of both Charisma House and *Charisma* magazine, wants to give you 3 FREE ISSUES of our award-winning magazine.

Since its inception in 1975, *Charisma* magazine has helped thousands of Christians stay connected with what God is doing worldwide.

Within its pages you will discover in-depth reports and the latest news from a Christian perspective, biblical health tips, global events in the body of Christ, personality profiles, and so much more. Join the family of *Charisma* readers who enjoy feeding their spirit each month with miracle-filled testimonies and inspiring articles that bring clarity, provoke prayer, and demand answers.

To claim your **3 free issues** of *Charisma*, send your name and address to: Charisma 3 Free Issue Offer, 600 Rinehart Road, Lake Mary, FL 32746. Or you may call 1-800-829-3346 and ask for Offer # 93FREE. This offer is only valid in the USA.

---

www.charismamag.com